VEGETABLES: 3-5 servings a day

FRUITS: 2-4 servings a day

Nutrition Education
Bahia Vista

GOOD ENOUGH TO EAT

A KID'S GUIDE TO FOOD AND NUTRITION

LIZZY ROCKWELL

HARPERCOLLINSPUBLISHERS

WAAAAH!

Babies cry when they're hungry.
Dogs bark and howl. When you feel hungry,
your stomach grumbles, your legs feel weak.
You don't cry or howl, but sometimes you feel cranky.

In the nick of time your dinner is ready. It looks
good, it smells good, it tastes good.

As soon as you eat, you feel better.

Hunger sends you strong signals. It lets you know that eating is the most important thing you do each day. The food you eat and drink keeps you alive. It builds, protects, and energizes your body.

Food makes you able to . . .

grow

think

breathe

move

stay cool

stay warm

fight germs

 AAAHCHOO!

heal

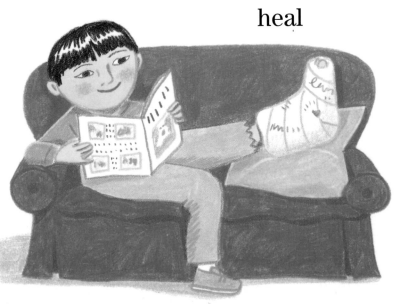

live!

Nutrients are the parts of food that your body uses to do its work. There are six different kinds of nutrients. You need large amounts of some nutrients and very small amounts of others in your diet.

Every food contains at least one nutrient, but healthy foods have lots of them. Your body uses different nutrients in different ways.

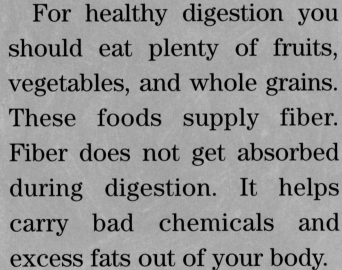

Digestion is the way food is broken down so that nutrients can be absorbed into your body.

For healthy digestion you should eat plenty of fruits, vegetables, and whole grains. These foods supply fiber. Fiber does not get absorbed during digestion. It helps carry bad chemicals and excess fats out of your body.

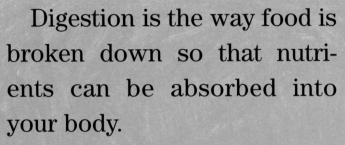

WHEN YOU DIGEST FOOD

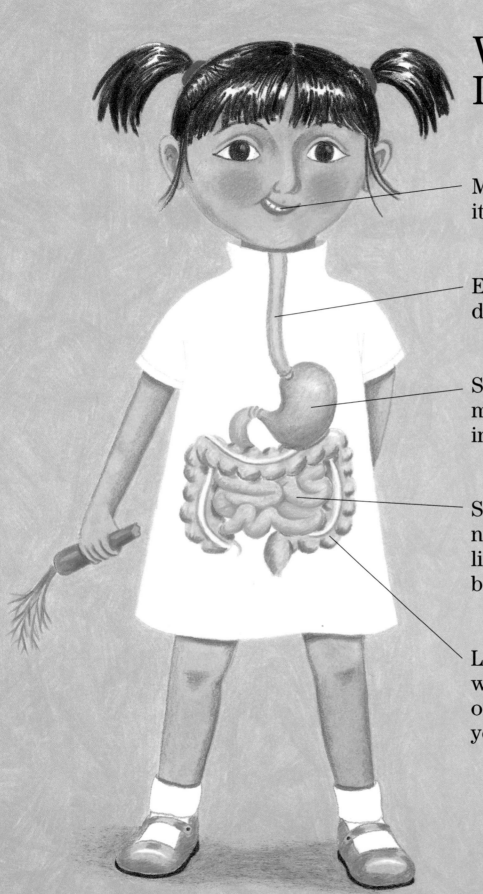

MOUTH grinds food and mixes it with saliva.

ESOPHAGUS pushes food down to your stomach.

STOMACH churns food and mixes it with acids. Turns food into a thick liquid.

SMALL INTESTINE absorbs nutrients through its spongy lining. Nutrients enter the bloodstream.

LARGE INTESTINE absorbs water and leads unused parts of food out of your body when you go to the toilet.

As soon as food is digested, nutrients start to work. Carbohydrates, protein, and fat get turned into energy. The amount of energy they supply is measured in calories. You use a lot of energy to run and play. You also use energy to stay warm, pump blood, breathe, think, heal, and grow.

Carbohydrates should supply most of the energy your body uses. You can detect carbohydrates in food just by taste. Foods that taste starchy or sweet contain carbohydrates.

Starchy foods give long-lasting energy.

Sweet foods give quick boosts of energy.

The energy from very sweet foods is used up very quickly.

Protein supplies energy. It also builds and repairs your muscles, skin, brain, blood, bones, and internal organs. You get protein when you eat animal foods, such as fish, meat, eggs, milk, and cheese.

You also get protein from plants. The parts of a plant that can sprout and grow, such as seeds, dry beans and peas, nuts, and grains, are good sources of protein.

Just as an old-fashioned lantern burns oil, you burn fat for heat and energy. Fat also helps make food taste good. But it is easy to eat too much fat. Fat has more calories than the other parts of food. If you eat more calories than you need, the unused calories are turned into body fat. Eating too many fatty foods can make you heavy.

Fat is in vegetable oil, butter, and cream. You can also see fat in the white and yellow parts of uncooked meat and chicken. Often, you cannot see the fat you are eating. To find out where fat is hiding, get a large piece of paper, a pencil, and samples of foods.

You don't need to worry about having too much water in your diet. Water is your body's main ingredient. Seventy percent of your body, including your blood, saliva, tears, urine, and sweat, is made with water.

Water escapes easily from your body. In a day you lose two cups of water just by breathing. When you cry, go to the bathroom, and sweat, you lose even more water. But as it leaves your body, water carries out wastes and cools you.

Vitamins and minerals are needed in tiny amounts to perform many important jobs in your body. They help all the nutrients in food work together.

Vitamins are found only in plants and animals.

B COMPLEX VITAMINS

Thiamin (B$_1$), Riboflavin (B$_2$), Niacin (B$_3$), Pantothenic Acid (B$_5$), Biotin, B$_6$, B$_{12}$, Folacin
Found in:

Minerals are tiny particles of rock and metal.

CALCIUM
Found in:

IRON   foods cooked in
Found in: iron pans

as well as:

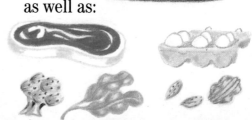

The best way to get all the vitamins and minerals you need is to eat a variety of fresh foods, including plenty of fruits and vegetables.

THE FOOD GUIDE PYRAMID

The Food Guide Pyramid shows you how many servings of different foods you should eat in a day. If you follow these guidelines, and drink plenty of water, you can get all the nutrients and fiber your body needs.

Fats, Oils, & Sweets:
Eat and use sparingly.

Milk, Yogurt, & Cheese:
3 Servings

Meat, Poultry, Fish, Dry Beans, Eggs, & Nuts:
2–3 Servings

Vegetables:
3–5 Servings

Fruits:
2–4 Servings

Bread, Cereal, Rice, & Pasta:
6–11 Servings

These foods are high in

FAT AND SUGAR

They have a lot of calories but not a lot of nutrients.
These foods should be eaten in small amounts.

These foods are good sources of

PROTEIN AND MINERALS

as well as vitamins, water, and fat.
Serving size: 2–3 oz. meat, fish, or poultry, 1 egg, $\frac{1}{2}$ cup beans,
2 tablespoons peanut butter, 1 cup milk or yogurt, 2 oz. cheese.

These foods are good sources of

VITAMINS, WATER, AND FIBER

as well as carbohydrates and minerals.
Serving size: $\frac{1}{2}$ cup chopped fruit or vegetables,
1 cup leafy vegetables, 1 piece of fruit, 1 melon wedge,
$\frac{3}{4}$ cup juice, $\frac{1}{4}$ cup dried fruit.

These foods are a good source of

CARBOHYDRATES

as well as vitamins, minerals, protein, and
fiber. Serving size: 1 slice bread, $\frac{1}{2}$ cup
cooked rice or pasta, 1 oz. dry cereal.

Source: U.S. Department of Agriculture.
U.S. Department of Health and Human Services.

Food keeps you alive, healthy, and strong.
It gives you energy and makes you grow.
Food is fun to make.

And food is fun to eat.

FULL O' BEANS SOUP (8 servings)

INGREDIENTS

1   cup dried white beans in enough water to cover beans by 2"
2   carrots
1   stalk celery
1   onion
5   cloves garlic
3   lean pork chops
1   can (14 ounces) diced plum tomatoes
1½   teaspoons salt
10   cups water
3   tablespoons olive oil
1   cup uncooked elbow pasta

1. The day before you make your soup, rinse the beans and soak them in a bowl with enough water to cover them by two inches. Cover the bowl and refrigerate it overnight.

2. The next day wash carrots and celery. Ask a grown-up to chop onion, celery, and carrots; peel garlic; and trim any visible fat from pork chops.

3. Drain the beans. Combine the beans, vegetables, garlic, pork chops, tomatoes, salt, and 10 cups water in a large soup pot.

4. Ask an adult to: place the soup pot over high heat and bring just to a boil; reduce the heat to medium low and simmer for 2½ hours; skim off any foam and fat that rise during cooking.

5. Ask a grown-up to remove the pork chops and 1 cup of cooked beans from the soup pot.

6. Mash the beans in a bowl with a fork until you make a mush. Ask an adult to put this mush back into the soup and stir.

7. Tear meat into little pieces when chops are cool enough to handle. Ask an adult to put meat into soup.

8. Add the olive oil and the pasta. Cook the soup 10 more minutes and serve.

Full o' Beans Soup supplies protein, water, carbohydrates, fat, Vitamin A, B vitamins, sodium, iron, and fiber. One portion contains 220 calories and gives you one serving each of these groups: meat/beans, vegetables, and grain.

ALPHABREAD (15–20 letters)

INGREDIENTS

1   package active dry yeast
2   tablespoons sugar
2½   cups warm water
3   tablespoons olive oil
6½   cups flour
2   teaspoons salt
      additional flour for work surface and hands
      additional olive oil for greasing bowl and cookie sheet
2   egg whites, whisked till frothy
      poppy seeds or sesame seeds

1. Combine the yeast, sugar, water, and olive oil in a very large mixing bowl. Let sit for 10 minutes.

2. Add 6½ cups flour and salt to the bowl. Stir with a spoon to combine. When the dough is too thick to stir, turn it onto a floured surface.

3. Dust your hands with flour. Knead dough: Push it away from you with the heels of your hands. Keeping hands dusted with flour, fold dough back on itself. Push it away again. After each foldover give dough a quarter turn. Continue to knead for about 10 minutes until dough is smooth and elastic.

4. Wash and dry bread bowl. Cover with thin layer of oil so that the bread does not stick to it. Put ball of dough into bowl. Cover with plastic wrap. Let dough rise in a warm place for two hours.

5. Preheat oven to 450°F.

6. Punch the dough down with your fist. Knead it a few times.

7. Pull off a piece of dough as big as an egg. Roll and stretch it into a long snake. Form the snake into letter shape. Do the same with rest of dough.

8. Place the shapes on a greased cookie sheet. Brush each shape with egg white and sprinkle with poppy or sesame seeds.

9. Ask an adult to: bake each batch of breads for about 10 minutes, until golden brown; remove from sheets immediately and serve warm.

Alphabread supplies carbohydrates, B vitamins, protein, sodium, and fat. One letter contains 150 calories and gives you one serving from the grain group.

LITTLE DIPPERS (8 servings)

INGREDIENTS

$\frac{1}{2}$ cup fat-free plain yogurt
$\frac{1}{2}$ cup nonfat sour cream
$\frac{1}{2}$ teaspoon garlic salt
3 dashes Tabasco sauce
4 stalks celery
1 red and 1 yellow pepper
1 bag peeled baby carrots
1 pint cherry tomatoes

1. Combine the yogurt, sour cream, garlic salt, and Tabasco sauce in a bowl. Mix together with a spoon. Cover the dip and store in the refrigerator while you prepare the vegetables.

2. Wash the vegetables. Ask an adult to cut the celery into sticks. Cut peppers in half. Remove stems and seeds. Cut halves into long, thin strips. Leave the carrots and tomatoes whole.

3. Arrange the vegetables on a platter with a bowl of dip in the center. Dip in!

Little Dippers supply Vitamins A and C, B vitamins, calcium, iron, potassium, sodium, water, protein, and fiber. One portion contains 75 calories, and gives you one serving from the vegetable group and a quarter serving from the dairy group.

FIZZADE (6 servings)

INGREDIENTS

2 cups lemonade
2 cups orange juice
2 cups seltzer or sparkling spring water
   slices of oranges and lemons

1. Combine lemonade, orange juice, and sparkling water in a pitcher with ice, and stir.

2. Decorate each glass with a lemon or orange slice.

Fizzade supplies water, Vitamin C, potassium, and carbohydrates. One portion contains about 70 calories, and gives you a half serving of fruit.

YOGI POPS (6 servings, 2 pops each)

INGREDIENTS

2 cups fat-free vanilla yogurt
10 strawberries, washed and with stems removed
1 banana in 6 pieces
$\frac{1}{2}$ cup pineapple juice

1. Combine all ingredients in a blender and blend on high until smooth and pink.

2. Pour the mixture into twelve 3-ounce paper cups. Place a Popsicle stick in the middle of each cup.

3. Cut out twelve 3-inch-square pieces of foil.

4. Poke a hole in the center of each piece of foil. Cover each cup with the foil while guiding the Popsicle stick through the hole. Crimp the foil around the edge of cup.

5. Place the cups in the freezer and freeze until solid. This will take around 6 hours.

6. Remove the foil and peel off the paper cup. Enjoy!

Yogi Pops supply calcium, Vitamin C, Vitamin D, potassium, carbohydrates, water, protein, and fiber. Two pops contain 110 calories and give you a half serving of dairy and a half serving of fruit.

MORE ABOUT CALORIES

Calories measure the amount of energy supplied by food. A teaspoon of fat has twice as many calories as a teaspoon of protein or carbohydrates. Vitamins, minerals, water, and fiber supply no calories.

Every day you should eat about as many calories as you use. This is easy if you avoid eating foods with a lot of fat or sugar and get plenty of exercise.

TO GET 200 CALORIES, YOU COULD EAT ONE OF THESE SERVINGS:

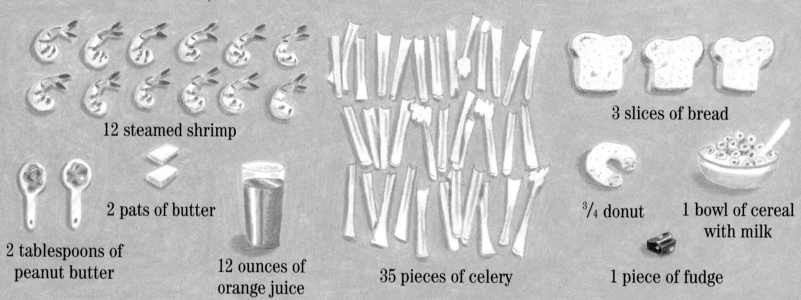

12 steamed shrimp

2 pats of butter

2 tablespoons of peanut butter

12 ounces of orange juice

35 pieces of celery

3 slices of bread

¾ donut

1 bowl of cereal with milk

1 piece of fudge

TO BURN 200 CALORIES YOU COULD:

run for ½ hour

walk for 1 hour

THIS IS GETTING BORING.

or sit perfectly still for 4 hours

For Annie, Nancy, and Phoebe

Thanks to Jodie Shield, MEd, RD, LD,
and Richard A. Manzi, MD,
for their help in reviewing this book.

The author used watercolors and colored pencils
on T.H. Saunders Hot Press Water Color paper
for the illustrations in this book.

Good Enough to Eat
A Kid's Guide to Food and Nutrition
Copyright © 1999 by Lizzy Rockwell
Manufactured in China. All rights reserved.
Visit our web site at http://www.harperchildrens.com.

Library of Congress Cataloging-in-Publication Data
Rockwell, Lizzy.
   Good enough to eat : a kid's guide to food and nutrition / Lizzy Rockwell.
     p.   cm.
   Summary: Describes the six categories of nutrients needed for good health,
how they work in the body, and what foods provide each.
   ISBN 0-06-027434-4. — ISBN 0-06-027435-2 (lib. bdg.)
   1. Nutrition—Juvenile literature.   2. Children—Nutrition—Juvenile literature.
[1. Food.]   I. Title.
QP141.R536   1999   97-32145
613.2—dc21   CIP
                                                                  AC

12 13 14 15 16 17 18 19 20

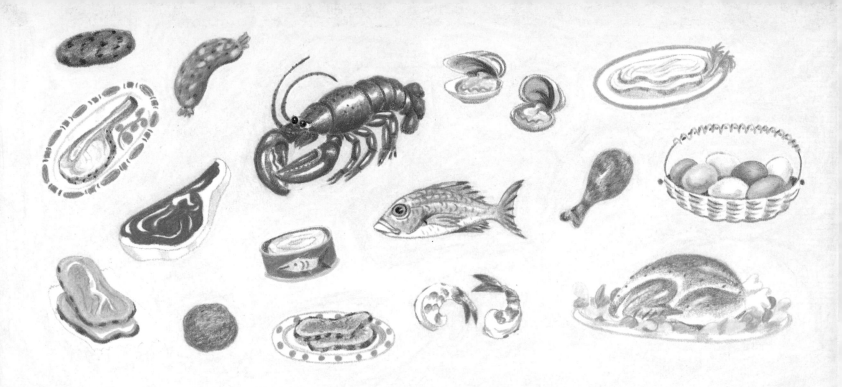

MEAT, POULTRY, FISH, EGGS,
DRY BEANS, and NUTS: 2-3 servings a day

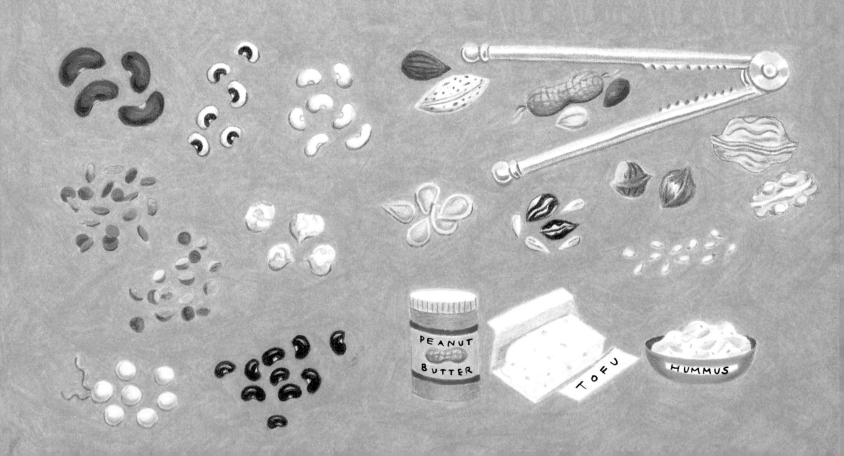